The Seven Deadly Sins of Legal Writing

The Seven Deadly Sins
of
Legal Writing

Theodore L. Blumberg

OWLWORKS

This guidebook has been undertaken by The Archangul Foundation:

Cataloguing information for this book is available from The Library of Congress

ISBNs: 1-934084-04-2
        978-1-934084-04-5

Owlworks is an imprint of The Archangul Foundation, Baltimore, MD

Typefaces: Chancery
          Book Antiqua

Printed by Thomson-Shore, Inc., Dexter, MI

For Mardi

Contents

The Seven Deadly Sins of Legal Writing

Legal writing, despite centuries of criticism (constructive and otherwise), remains steadfastly awful. Legal prose tends to be pompous, antiquated, and opaque; redundant and full of jargon, bloated like a corpse and infused with a gray, stultifying dullness that passes for dignity. When you consider that what most lawyers mostly do is write—letters, memoranda, contracts, briefs, wills, email—this is startling. No other profession would tolerate, let alone tacitly endorse, execrable work.

Many lawyers, perhaps even most lawyers, admit there's a problem. Few will admit that they might be contributing to it. As a colleague of mine once put it, "I never met a man who didn't think he was a great lover or a lawyer who didn't think he was a great writer. Ninety-nine times out of a hundred they're deluded."

The cure—at least with regard to becoming a better legal writer—is quite easy. Anyone, given a basic level of literacy, can become a competent writer. Almost everyone can become a good writer, a clear writer. One of the surest ways to improve is by simply avoiding the bad habits that clog legal writing. By "not doing," by refusing to yield to the temptation to try to "sound like a lawyer," most of us can significantly improve our writing almost immediately. The tougher battle is overcoming the profession's entrenched affinity for prose that's deliberately opaque and dreadful. And while I will present some theories about why we lawyers love bad prose, my objective in writing this handbook is to isolate from a multitude of sins several of the most egregious, most common, and most easy to avoid (or rather, renounce).

Permit me to introduce The Seven Deadly Sins of Legal Writing.

The First Deadly Sin: Passivity

While legal education in America is famous for fostering assertiveness (some would say aggression), it also fosters a preference for the passive voice. In legal prose the passive voice is truly ubiquitous. "The agreement was entered into by the purchaser," "the child was injured by the defective toy," "the plea agreement was approved by the court," "the young woman was solicited by the Governor."

The natural construction, the obvious construction, is "The purchaser entered into the agreement," "the defective toy injured the child," "the court approved the plea agreement," and so on. As Strunk & White point out in *The Elements of Style*, the active voice is usually to be preferred because it's direct and vigorous: "I shall always remember my first visit to Boston," is better than "My first visit to Boston will always be remembered by me."[1]

Of course, as legal writers we're not interested in style for style's sake. Legal writing, whatever literary merit it might contain, must be utilitarian as a wrench; it's meant to be *used*. Whether an opinion letter, a will, or a construction agreement offer esthetic pleasure is beside the point. If they don't serve their respective purposes they are useless.

The cure is clarity. To be useful, legal writing must be clear.

---

1. William Strunk, Jr. & E.B. White, *The Elements of Style* 18 (1979).

Style is essential to the extent it fosters clarity. Which brings me back to the passive voice.

The passive voice usually impedes clarity because it fights the way we naturally process language. Comprehension depends on the reader's ability to translate words into images and ideas. By detaching syntax from the way it is most readily understood — as a meaningful sequence of events — the passive voice often slows comprehension.[2] "The ball was thrown by the quarterback" makes the reader work to associate the words with the things they signify and then rearrange the sentence so it can be apprehended as a logical sequence of events. "The quarterback threw the ball" is immediately understandable. It's clear.

The active voice orders ideas in the way in which native speakers of English most readily comprehend them. "When you use a verb in the active voice, the subject of the sentence does the acting. 'John kicks the ball.'"[3] In other words, "its syntax meets the English-speaker's expectation that the subject of a sentence will perform the action of the verb."[4]

And it just sounds better. As William Zinsser, one of the very best writers about writing put it:

"Joe saw him" is strong. "He was seen by Joe" is weak. The first is short and precise; it leaves no doubt about who did what. The second is necessarily longer and it has an insipid quality: something was done by somebody to someone else ... A style that consists of passive constructions will sap the reader's energy. Nobody ever quite knows what is being perpetrated by whom and on whom.[5]

---

2. *See* Bryan A. Garner, *Legal Writing in Plain English* 25 (2001).
3. Richard C. Wydick, *Plain English for Lawyers* 29 (1998).
4. Garner at 25.
5. William Zinsser, *On Writing Well* 68 (1998).

In addition to its other virtues, the active voice, as Zinsser notes, makes for shorter, terser sentences.[6] Anything that eliminates unnecessary words is to be valued. Unnecessary words are clutter. The active voice, with its natural ordering of syntax and its tendency to promote concision, is a valuable weapon in the fight for clarity.

So with all of that going for it, why do lawyers so often favor the passive voice instead of the active voice?

There are at least several reasons, one of which is habit. Bad writing begets bad writing. So much legal prose is written in the passive voice that lawyers unconsciously assume there must be something to it, that that's the right way to write. Before long, the passive voice becomes second nature.

Additionally, because it imparts a sense of stuffiness and formality, some lawyers treasure the odor of antiquity the passive voice can provide; it's like coating your sentences in gray flannel. In a profession that reveres precedent, antiquity provides a sense of security: if the document sounds like it was exhumed from the tomb of the Unknown Barrister, it must be authentic and correct.

Lawyers also favor the passive voice for the very qualities that militate against it. We often write in a state of angst, frightened of making plain statements. If things go wrong and we need wiggle room, what will we do? There won't be a jungle of words in which to hide. Often in this profession, everything we write is freighted with the potential for disaster — at least that's how it feels. And much of our writing is done with others — senior partners, judges,

---

6. *Id. See also* Strunk & White at 19 ("when a sentence is made stronger [through using the active voice] it usually becomes shorter ... brevity is a by-product of vigor."); Garner at 25 ("[the active voice] usually requires fewer words").

clients—all of whom believe themselves to be pocket Hemingways—looking over our shoulder. As a wise man once said, "The strongest instinct in humankind isn't self-preservation; it's the urge to change someone else's copy."

To maintain an illusion of pliancy, to hedge a little or a lot, agreements are entered into by the parties, firearms are discharged by perpetrators, and he was seen by Joe.

The Case for Passivity

Every rule has its exceptions. Now that I've vilified the passive voice, let's talk about when it can and should be used.

1. To Create Ambiguity

Transactional lawyers often want a degree of ambiguity and abstraction in a document to create "wiggle room" the client might need. The passive voice is a good tool for this, particularly when combined with abstract words (discussed below). Skillfully deployed, the passive voice is better than fine print for hiding terms the writer wants to conceal or at least not draw attention to. (I leave to a CLE course on legal ethics the question of whether this kind of thing is permissible. For now let's acknowledge that it's done, that it's often considered part and parcel of skillful drafting, and leave it at that.) The truth is, there are times when lawyers want to be anything but clear. Just as lawyers used to hide a troublesome document by putting it in the middle of thousands of pages of innocuous material that would be produced to the other side, some drafters cloak potentially controversial provisions in the passive voice and put them in the middle of dense documents.

The hope is that by the time readers get to it, their morale will have buckled and they won't have the wherewithal to decipher it. Moral: when you don't want clarity, consider the passive voice.

2. *To Underscore a Word*

Skillful brief writers avoid the excessive underscoring or italicizing of words for emphasis.[7] (Some lawyers have taken to using bold italics *to make sure the reader gets the point!*)

The passive voice, properly used, can throw a spotlight on a word or phrase you want to emphasize without resorting to italics. "The poison was administered by the attendant," highlights "poison" in a sentence in which italicizing the word would look strange. "The perjured testimony was repeated by the plaintiff on cross," underscores "perjured testimony" without underscoring.

While the passive voice is no substitute for italics when only italics will do, those occasions are less common than one might think; so use italics *sparingly* and consider the passive voice.

3. *To Drain Emotion from your Writing*

Litigators use the passive voice to take the emotional charge out of ugly facts. "Defendant Faber had three beers, left the bar, got into his Pathfinder and started driving up Lexington Avenue. At

---

7. Frederick Wiener, whose extraordinary *Effective Appellate Advocacy* is finally back in print after decades in book limbo, counsels that "A sound general rule is to use italics sparingly ... used too freely in the text of a brief, they are apt to be regarded as ... insults to any reader's intelligence. It is perfectly possible to write a strong, forceful, even a fighting brief, without a single word italicized for emphasis." Frederick B. Wiener, *Effective Appellate Advocacy* 148 (Christopher T. Lutz & William Pannill, eds., A.B.A. 2004).

40th Street he ran a red light and slammed into Kyle Chan as the boy was crossing the street on his skateboard. According to witnesses, Chan flew into the air, crashed onto the Pathfinder's windshield, shattering it, and fell to the ground."

Let's say you represent Faber. Your characterization of the facts will be quite different. You'll want to be passive and abstract. "Several beers were consumed at the bar by Mr. Faber. A quarter of an hour later, at approximately 5 p.m., as the intersection of Lexington Avenue and 40th Street was approached by his vehicle, the traffic light turned from yellow to red. Tragically, at that moment the decedent skated into the crosswalk on his skateboard. Unable to stop his vehicle in time, the intersection was entered by the vehicle, and the decedent was struck by the vehicle."

The passage is noticeably longer in the second version, and part of that length is caused by the passive voice. Note, too, the juxtaposition of the passive voice ("as the intersection ... was approached by his vehicle") with the active voice ("the traffic light turned from yellow to red.") The passive voice slows the action, the active speeds it up to create the impression that the light changed abruptly. The overall effect of the second version, though it's admittedly heavy-handed in its use of the passive voice to illustrate the point, is to distance the reader from the squeal of brakes, the thudding crack of steel against flesh and bone, the sound of shattering glass, and the soft thud of a body falling to the asphalt.

Film directors use different speeds, lenses, and angles. Lawyers have words, words, words, but words are more than enough. This, after all, is the point of rhetoric, an unjustly maligned term of late[8]

---

8. *See* Brian Vickers, *In Defence of Rhetoric* viii, 1 (1988); Richard A. Posner, *Cardozo: A Study in Reputation* 54 (1990).

that is at the heart of what we do as advocates. It's not what you say; it's how you say it.

The Second Deadly Sin: Abstraction

*L*aws are created to control behavior; that's their purpose. So when you write a legal document, remember that it's supposed to guide how people act. Since mere mortals have to make use of it, it helps if we can understand it.

Like a supplicant consulting an oracle, I took the CPLR from the shelf and let it open at random. Rule 8600 was my reward — to wit:

It is the intent of this article, which may hereafter be known and cited as the "New York State Equal Access to Justice Act," to create a mechanism authorizing the recovery of counsel fees and other reasonable expenses in certain actions against the State of New York ...

"Create a mechanism" is fine if you're a watchmaker. If you're a lawyer, it's doubletalk. "Certain actions"? Tell us which ones. And note the passive voice and use of pathetic fallacy to suggest the Article has intent rather than its drafters. Here it is in plain English:

This Article authorizes the recovery of attorneys' fees and other reasonable expenses in the following kinds of actions against the State of New York ...

If the revision strikes you as too plain, too clear to be trusted, keep in mind the observation of appellate specialist Christopher Lutz: "You are no less a lawyer for being understandable."[9]

Concrete language conveys the sense of real people doing things—leaving property to their children, selling a business, proving they were in Cleveland when the victim was murdered in Astoria. Because we deal in the practical, our writing should be vivid yet plain, clear and concise. A good test is to ask yourself, when reading something you've written, if you can picture the events you've written about. "Anticipatory repudiation" sounds important but I can't conjure an image of what it means to flesh-and-blood people. Tell me Ajax, Ltd. was habitually paying your client's bills three to six months late, which led your client to suspect that Ajax was about to founder, so she canceled Ajax's contract to prevent losing money. That I can picture.

Shun abstraction in favor of the concrete. We help people do what they need or want to do. Our language should be plain and practical as hardware, and as quietly handsome in its unadorned way.

---

9. Quoted in Bryan A. Garner, *The Redbook: A Manual on Legal Style* 160 (2nd ed. 2006).

The Third Deadly Sin: Adverbiage

Every law student learns to avoid "clearly," as in "Clearly, the agreement was void from the outset." Too bad "significantly," "incredibly," "undoubtedly," "erroneously," "fallaciously," etc. aren't also singled out. They occur in legal writing with annoying frequency, often as the first word of a sentence: "Significantly, the agreement was modified after Barnes had signed it ..." "Incredibly, the Government contends that the search was justified by exigent circumstances ..." "Undoubtedly, the rubber ducky was dangerous when it came off the assembly line, and the manufacturer clearly knew of the danger ..."

Indiscriminate use of adverbs, like overindulgence in italics, insults the reader's intelligence.[10] If your point is significant or fallacious, clear or credible, there is no reason to shout. Adverbiage, as I call it, creates resistance in readers to the very conclusion you would like them to draw. This is particularly true of judges, who wade through brief after brief in which lazy lawyers, rather than making the points plain through careful writing, take the adverbial shortcut and sabotage themselves. Allowing readers to conclude from the undisputed facts that your point is incredible or significant is more powerful than trying to force it upon them by auctorial fiat.

---

10. *See* Wiener, *Effective Appellate Advocacy,* at 148.

Adverbs also tend to weaken your point by clumsily foreshadowing it to the reader. When the point about to be made is surprising or startling, the adverb ruins the surprise by tipping the writer's hand, which is why good novelists rarely foreshadow important events with adverbs. Here's the last paragraph of J.D. Salinger's short story, *A Perfect Day for Bananafish:*

He glanced at the girl lying asleep on one of the twin beds, then he went over to one of the pieces of luggage, opened it, and from under a pile of shorts and undershirts he took out an Ortgies calibre 7.65 automatic. He released the magazine, looked at it, then reinserted it. He cocked the piece. Then he went over and sat down on the unoccupied twin bed, looked at the girl, aimed the pistol, and fired a bullet through his right temple.

Here's the passage as it might appear as part of the facts section of a brief:

Stealthily, he glanced at the girl lying asleep on one of the twin beds, then he quietly went over to one of the pieces of luggage, opened it, and from under a pile of shorts and undershirts he carefully took out an Ortgies calibre 7.65 automatic. He released the magazine, looked at it, then reinserted it. Significantly, he cocked the piece. Incredibly, then he went over and sat down on the unoccupied twin bed, looked at the girl, aimed the pistol, and tragically fired a bullet through his right temple.

Most of us don't like to be told what to think or feel. This goes double for lawyers and judges, who are trained to read with a skeptical eye and varying degrees of scrutiny. Go over your writing with pen in hand and circle the adverbs. Determine whether you're taking adverbial shortcuts because you haven't bothered to make the point through careful writing, or whether the adverbs

---

11. J.D. Salinger, *A Perfect Day for Bananafish,* in *Nine Stories* 26 (1953).

are useful. When in doubt, make significant points significant through content and context and let readers discover the significance on their own.

Exceptions

Inevitably, there are times when adverbs are welcome.

1. When They Convey Information

"Statistically," "Nearly," "Economically" are all fine ways to start a sentence. They alert the reader that facts are coming. They don't try to guide a response.

2. To Dissipate Emotion

The section on the passive voice contains the following sentence: "Tragically, at that moment the decedent skated into the crosswalk on his skateboard." By foreshadowing the collision "Tragically" beats us to the emotional punch. It's what a child does when she tells her parents she has a confession that's going to make them very, very angry, and admits she ate the cookies. Or what a good advocate does by eliciting facts harmful to her case before the adversary brings them out. Each warning of what's to come inoculates the audience.

The same is true of adverbs. "Significantly" takes some significance out of the significant event it presages. "Remarkably" tends to make the event that follows not so remarkable after all. Here's a paragraph by Raymond Carver:

Just as he started to turn off the lamp, he thought he saw something in the hall. He kept staring and thought he saw it again, a pair of small eyes. His heart turned. He blinked and kept staring. He leaned over to look for something to throw. He picked up one of his shoes. He sat up straight and held the shoe with both hands. He heard her snoring and set his teeth. He waited. He waited for it to move once more, to make the slightest noise.[12]

Now let's put in some adverbs: "Frighteningly [or "Eerily"], just as he started to turn off the lamp, he thought he saw something in the hall. Wordlessly, he kept staring ... Awfully, his heart turned ...″

And suddenly the tension evaporates. The ominous feeling the paragraph conveyed dissolves in adverbiage. A verbal tool so effective at killing emotion is worth using—when you want to lessen the emotional impact the words will have on the reader. Adverbs are the wide-angle lenses and extreme close-ups of language. Sparingly used, they can be effective. Clumsily deployed, they turn prose into clunky melodrama.

---

12. Raymond Carver, *What's in Alaska?* in *Will You Please Be Quiet, Please?* 93 (1992).

The Fourth Deadly Sin: Verbosity, or "Blumberg's Rule of Infliction"

Think of every brief you file as an infliction.

Judges don't read our briefs because they look interesting or have flashy covers with imaginative illustrations of contracts being sundered, marriages destroyed by adulterous trysts or patents being infringed by unscrupulous upstarts. There is no author photo on the back cover with a brief bio:

Janet Hastings, a partner at Childs, Resnor and Calabash, lives in Alexandria, Virginia with her husband Tom and their sons Peter and Raoul. A recipient of the National Advocacy Foundation's award for groundbreaking work on federal jurisdiction, this is her fifth brief on the Commerce Clause.

Judges read our briefs (at least we hope they read them) because they have to.

Can you remember the first time you were assigned homework? The first time you understood that school didn't end when the bell rang at three? That's the feeling judges get when they receive a tome of words. It's the feeling partners get when they receive a twenty-page memo. It's the feeling clients get when they receive a ten-page opinion letter.

It's easy to overlook the fact that judges don't look forward to reading briefs the way I hurry home from Barnes & Noble with a new Richard Ford. I might be proud of my well-argued brief about how a film distributor engaged in deceptive accounting and breached her contract with my client, but I have no illusions that the judge is going to take it to the beach instead of the latest Stephen King. Alexander Bickel's brief in the Pentagon Papers case is a masterpiece.[13] But it wouldn't be in my bag for the flight to Sydney.

In short, write short. Never use fewer words than necessary but never use more. A ten-page brief is more likely to be read, and more likely to be carefully read, than a brief three times as long. If a hundred pages are required to cover the topic at hand, so be it. But if it can be cut to seventy-five, start slashing. Brevity is the soul of wit and your reader's best friend. I've often wished what I were reading were shorter. Rarely have I wished it longer.

Readers have an attention span of about 30 seconds.[14] Edit ruthlessly. Most first drafts can be cut by 50 percent without losing any information.[15] Cut the underemployed words, superfluous citations, and needlessly repeated ideas. If you still produce a long document, you'll know every word is earning its keep.

One good way to edit is by putting in brackets every word and phrase that's likely expendable.[16] Re-read the piece and skip the material. Repeat the process. More can almost always be cut. Pay close attention to long sentences (any sentence of thirty or more words). They often form verbal labyrinths the reader will get lost in.

---

13. *N.Y. Times Co. v. United States*, 403 U.S. 713, 91 S. Ct. 2140 (1971). The brief, along with other superb appellate briefs, is available from The Professional Education Group, Inc. 800.229.CLE1.

14. Zinsser, *On Writing Well*, at 9.

15. *Id.* at 17.

16. *Id.* at 17–18.

When you're in the initial stages of writing, write to your heart's content. Get it all on the page, every idea. That's no time to be an editor. First drafts, as Hemingway once put it, are always garbage. (Though he didn't use the word "garbage.") Then start reordering and trimming. When you have your second or third draft, start cutting and keep cutting. Good writing makes every word count. Here's a paragraph from George Orwell's essay, *Politics and the English Language.* See if you can find extraneous words.

Most people who bother about the matter at all would admit that the English language is in a bad way, but it is generally assumed that we cannot by conscious action do anything about it. Our civilization is decadent and our language — so the argument runs — must inevitably share in the general collapse. It follows that any struggle against the abuse of language is a sentimental archaism, like preferring candles to electric light or hansom cabs to aeroplanes. Underneath this lies the half-conscious belief that language is a natural growth and not an instrument which we shape for our own purposes.[17]

From V.S. Naipaul, who's fastidious about word-clutter, here's the second paragraph of his essay *Steinbeck in Monterey:*

Cannery Row in Monterey, the one John Steinbeck wrote about, disfigures a pretty California coastline. The canneries used to can sardines; but the sardines began to disappear from Monterey Bay not long after Steinbeck published his book in 1945; and today all but one of the canneries have closed down. The cannery buildings remain, where they have not been destroyed by fire: white corrugated-iron buildings, as squat and plain as warehouses, backing out into the sea over a low cliff, braced by timber and tons of concrete which

---

17. George Orwell, *Politics and the English Language,* in *A Collection of Essays* 156 (1981).

now only blasting can remove. Some are abandoned and show broken windows; some are warehouses; some have been converted into restaurants, boutiques, gift-shops.[18]

The Orwell passage is an example of a writer spinning an argument without a superfluous word or idea. The Naipaul exemplifies a writer stating facts vividly, engagingly, and concisely.

Here's a passage from a factual statement in a brief written by a law firm that ranks as one of the top ten firms in the country. I've bracketed unnecessary words and changed the names of the parties:

In June 2002, HYZ terminated Smith [from his employment as a senior auditor and assistant vice-president] based on the deterioration of his [job] performance over [a period of] several years. In November 2004, Smith commenced an arbitration before the New York Stock Exchange seeking [both] compensatory and punitive damages based on allegations that he was [wrongfully] discharged because he [had] detected money laundering in HYZ's Chicago office. Smith also sought compensation for consulting services he provided to HYZ after his termination. On March 1, 2005 [in connection with the arbitration] Smith and HYZ entered into a confidentiality agreement concerning any documents from HYZ [that were] in Smith's possession, [as well as discovery material exchanged in the course of the arbitration] ...

The passage is full of redundancy. Smith was terminated. Leaving aside the question whether "discharged" or "fired" would be a better verb, we know he was terminated *from his employment*. We know what deteriorated was his *job* performance as opposed to, say, his acumen playing spoons. If he seeks compensatory

---

18. V.S. Naipaul, *Steinbeck in Monterey*, in *The Writer and the World* 334 (2002).

and punitive damages, *both* is unnecessary. Cutting "wrongfully" eliminates a needless word and sharpens the issue: the reader will be prompted to wonder, "Is it against the law to fire someone who finds out his employer is committing a crime?"

When it comes to verbosity, judicial opinions are some of the worst offenders. Apart from the needless repetition of the same ideas three and four times, the use of three words where one will do, passive constructions, and liberal doses of jargon, opinions often get off to a stultifying start with a litany of procedural jabber. Lawyers would be well advised to avoid the throat clearing before getting to it, as would many judges. If you find that you can't get to the heart of the matter without a prolix warm-up, fine. Write the gray introductory prose that no one pays attention to. Then cut it. It's unnecessary. Here's the opening sentence of a recent opinion from the Supreme Court of the United States: "Petitioner Michael Crawford stabbed a man who allegedly tried to rape his wife, Sylvia."[19] No procedural jabber or throat clearing. Justice Scalia, one of the most gifted legal writers, gets to it. That opening sentence tells us what we need to know about the background. Its concision reassures us that the decision will get to the points and stick to them. We know that we're in the hands of a masterful stylist. From the opening sentence, our interest is engaged and the writer's credibility is established.

Make your points clearly and as quickly as possible. Strive to be brief. Robert Frost's advice to poets (or maybe it was Gertrude Stein to Hemingway) is also good for lawyers: "Concentrate, concentrate, concentrate."

---

19. *Crawford v. Wash.*, 124 S.Ct. 1354, 1356 (2004).

The Fifth Deadly Sin: Redundancy

A sin that's closely related to Verbosity, Redundancy is one of the chief causes of wordiness, particularly when it takes the form of pleonasm or tautology, the needless use of two or more words to say the same thing ("baby puppies," "wet water," "terrible tragedy"). I used to think this was a disease that targeted lawyers. Then Professor DeAnn DeLuna, who teaches literature at Johns Hopkins University, alerted me to the fact that lawyers used to be paid by the word:

It has been the custom in modern Europe to regulate, upon most occasions, the payment of the attornies and clerks of court according to the number of pages which they had occasion to write; the court, however, requiring that each page should contain so many lines, and each line so many words. In order to increase their payment, the attornies and clerks have contrived to multiply words beyond all necessity, to the corruption of the law language of, I believe, every court of justice in Europe.[20]

Now I suspect that our fondness for pleonasm and verbosity is a holdover. Whatever the origin, it's a habit to be shaken.

One way to eliminate redundancy is by avoiding what Bryan

---

20. Adam Smith, *The Wealth of Nations*, Book 5, at 88 (1st ed., 1776).

Garner calls "doublets" and "triplets."[21] "Cease and desist," "Indemnify and hold harmless." A common triplet is "give, devise, and bequeath." These should be removed from our forms, our writing, and our sensibility.

Another form of redundancy is "The Needlessly Repeated Title."

Let's say you open a letter from a lawyer. Centered and in bold, underscored for good measure, it says:

<u>Re: Roberts v. Private Reserve, Inc., Case no. 8799/06 (Shirer. J.)</u>

Then comes the opening sentence: "I am writing with regard to the above-referenced action ..."

What else would the letter be about? The "Re:" line gave it away. Get on with it. After the salutation ("Dear Mrs. Tanzanite") jump in: "The court has scheduled a preliminary conference for May 1 at 2 p.m."

The Needlessly Repeated Title is nearly always seen in briefs. A lawyer files a brief with the title "Plaintiff's Memorandum of Law in Support of Her Motion for Sanctions because of Defendant's Spoliation of Evidence." Nine times out of ten the brief's opening sentence will be something like "Plaintiff Sheila Squeri, through her counsel, respectfully submits this Memorandum of Law in support of her motion for sanctions due to defendant Michaels' spoliation of evidence." A wordy, stultifying and pointless way to make a first impression.

Let the title do the job. Use your first sentence to grab the reader's attention: "When Michael Smith, the defendant's Director of Compliance, received the Complaint, which was filed on

---

21. Garner, *The Redbook*, at 192–94.

December 4, 2006, he pulled Ms. Squeri's personnel file, took out her memoranda to the company's President, in which she complained that Smith was sexually harassing her, and shredded them."

In *Tristram Shandy*, Laurence Sterne satirizes legal writing by including a contract brimming with tautologies. Shandy was published in 1760 but its parody of legal writing looks like contracts and forms that cross my desk every week. The editor of my edition states, "The ... contract parodies legal language that says the same thing as many different ways as possible in an attempt to keep slippery life under control ..."[22] (See Appendix.)

Well, that's the point. Slippery life is so slippery that trying to control it with language — let alone redundant language — is a fool's errand. Look at the thousands of lawsuits over documents that were full of doublets and triplets and all the boilerplate that has failed the test of time. Needlessly repeating the same idea in different words doesn't make your case stronger, just longer. Renounce Redundancy.

---

22. Laurence Sterne, *Tristram Shandy* 27–28, n. 4 (Howard Anderson, ed., 1980).

The Sixth Deadly Sin: Speaking Footnotes

Footnotes intrude and distract. They're a phone that won't stop ringing.

I mean speaking footnotes, the ones that create digressive blocks of text at the bottom of the page. As Frederick Wiener put it, "Perhaps no single implement of all the vast apparatus of scholarship is so thoroughly misused in the law as the footnote. There may be some justification in ... the academic world for that formidable display of learning and industry, the thin stream of text meandering in a vale of footnotes, but that sort of thing is quite self-defeating in the law: because it makes the writer's thoughts more difficult to follow — and hence far less likely to persuade the judicial reader."[23]

True, there are legal writers who use footnotes beautifully. Herald Price Fahringer comes to mind. Laurence Tribe. Judge Calabresi here in the Second Circuit. Their footnotes amplify instead of distracting. That level of skill with footnotes is attainable but it takes some thought and some practice. Too often, footnotes are used to engage in flashy displays of erudition, or to try to hide material harmful to your case, or to try to beat the page limits.

Whenever you feel tempted to use a speaking footnote, ask yourself if the information is indipensable. If the answer is yes,

---

23. Wiener, *Effective Appellate Advocacy,* at 145.

put it in the text. If no, cut it. If the information falls somewhere between useless and essential—if it's truly helpful to the reader but just doesn't belong in the text—then consider relegating it to a footnote.[24]

Using footnotes for citations, on the other hand, is an excellent idea. Bryan Garner suggests putting every citation in a footnote to avoid distracting islands of citations that interrupt the text.[25] The reason briefs, memoranda and letters contain citations in the text, Garner explains, is purely technological. For decades, those documents were prepared on typewriters. Whereas law review articles, scholarly works and just about every other kind of document that uses footnotes were professionally typeset.

If you've ever tried to draft footnotes on a typewriter, you know how hellish an experience it is. If you've never had the pleasure, imagine massaging your scalp with a broken bottle. So to spare the typist, the convention of putting citations into the text was devised. It was purely an accommodation, a trade-off. Now that computers can add as many footnotes as you like, there is no longer any reason to adhere to an obsolete convention. Try Garner's approach. It's nice and sleek and easy on the eyes.

---

24. I went through this with footnote 7. The language was too important to omit, but it seemed out of place in the text, too digressive. I tried to make it fit there but it was the proverbial square peg. Since I didn't have other speaking footnotes in this piece, I indulged myself and included one. Now here's another. Distracting, isn't it?

25. Garner, *The Winning Brief* 114–19 (1999). See also William Glaberson, *Legal Citations on Trial in Innovation v. Tradition*, N.Y. Times, July 8, 2001, at A1 (discussing the profession's response to Garner's suggestion that all citations be relegated to footnotes).

The Seventh Deadly Sin: Negativity

Our minds have a hard time comprehending something that isn't. Linguists and psychologists posit that the unconscious is incapable of grasping the negative; the negative part of the statement remains unprocessed.[26] Doctors versed in hypnotherapy frequently give patients directives loaded with double-negatives. Because the unconscious can't grasp them, the conscious mind has to untangle the meaning, which distracts the patient while suggestions directed to the unconscious can be embedded in the doctor's speech.[27] So if you're a doctor trying to induce a light trance, double-negatives are not entirely unhelpful if you don't want the patient not to stop focusing on what you aren't offering to his conscious mind.

If you're a lawyer, double-negatives are verbal algebra. But they're often used in legal writing. Here's a quote from a recent decision I found while leafing through the *Law Journal:* "The government has not contested that a claim of ineffective assistance of counsel is not procedurally barred by the failure to raise it on direct appeal, nor could it."[28] Why not "A claim of ineffective assis-

26. *See, e.g.* Milton H. Erickson, M.D. and Ernest L. Rossi, *Hypnotherapy, An Exploratory Casebook* 153 (1992).

27. *Id.*

28. *Graziose v. United States,* 2004 WL 1194590, at *5 (S.D.N.Y June 1, 2004).

tance of counsel is not procedurally barred by the failure to raise it on direct appeal, nor could it." Or "A claim of ineffective assistance of counsel may be raised in a habeas petition whether or not it was raised on direct appeal."? Byran Garner gives this example:

A member who has no fewer than 25 years of credited service but has not yet attained the age of 60 years and is not eligible for retirement may not voluntarily retire early without first filing a written application with the board.[29]

The clause revised:

Even if you're a member who is not otherwise eligible for retirement, you may voluntarily retire if you are under the age of 60 and have at least 25 years of credited service. To do this, you must file a written application with the board.

Use a double-negative and you give the reader a puzzle. If the reader wanted a puzzle, she'd likely peruse math texts, crosswords, or murder mysteries set in places with names like Derbyshire. Change double-negatives to positive statements. Instead of saying swimming is not prohibited, tell us it's allowed. If settlement is not unlikely, say it's likely or probable. Even single-negatives should be made into positive statements. "At Ramsdale Ltd., office romances are not encouraged" is nice and coy. Who needs nice and coy in an employee handbook? "At Ramsdale Ltd., office romances are discouraged."

Sometimes one has to grit the teeth, gather the courage, and make a positive statement in a simple declarative sentence.

---

29. Garner, *Legal Writing,* at 30.

Exceptions

Double-negatives are not entirely unuseful, however. They're good for establishing nuances and shades of meaning. "The dentist made sure that during the root canal, the patient was not uncomfortable." No sane person is comfortable during a root canal. (Some of us say the rosary, take to drink, or insist on the strongest possible gases and humors for a routine cleaning. Not me, of course, but some.) To say the patient was comfortable would be an overstatement. "Not uncomfortable" is a twilight state between relaxation and white-knuckled terror. The double-negative is the most accurate way of conveying it.

Double-negatives are also good for imparting an arch, understated, or ironic tone: "Last week, Harry and Marge Jebib of Park Slope won four million dollars during a trip to Las Vegas. Harry, a New York City public school teacher with a taste for understatement and a baby on the way, said the money was 'not unwelcome.'"

Hunt through your writing for double-negatives. Change them into positive statements. Save the negativity — double or single — for situations rich in ambiguity or awash in irony.

Conclusion

1 had dinner with a close friend who's also a client. We talked about a legal question he'd hired me to answer. After researching the issue I sent him an opinion letter. I asked if he'd read it. He had. I asked if he understood it and said my question wasn't meant as an insult; some of the issues were tough. He said it was the only letter from a lawyer he's ever read all the way through — and understood. I was flattered. He's dealt with his share of attorneys. I asked, "Why don't you read letters from lawyers?"

He said, "They're impossible to decipher. Lawyers don't write for people. They write for each other."

He's right.

And if you write clear, durable prose you'll likely be viewed as a heretic. At many firms new associates who write well despite law school often find that their work is revised (that is, corrupted) until it's got the ring of legalese. Prose that would pass muster in *The Wall Street Journal, The New York Times,* or *The New Yorker* would likely be viewed as crude and undignified by many a lawyer, who would want to gild it with jargon and a big dose of incomprehensibility. Of course this is self-defeating. Legalese disguises sloppy thinking and fools not only the client but the lawyer who wrote it into believing she's said something of substance. Only in the legal profession is clear and plain English considered subversive.

This is traceable to envy of the guilds and other professions, which used tools and materials beyond the ability of the untrained. A mason lays bricks, a surgeon wields a scalpel, a lawyer has only words — common property — to accomplish her work. To instill in the public a sense that we're as necessary and as highly trained (despite our lack of gleaming instruments and oddly-shaped tools) as the smith, the surgeon, the cable guy, we've developed arcane jargon and oblique prose; we *want* to convey the appearance of membership in an elite group that communicates in ways inaccessible to the laity. We're afraid that to write plain English is to lift the curtain and expose the Wizard as nothing special. All of which is unnecessary and a trifle absurd. People hire us for our minds, our knowledge, our ability to find out what the law was, is, and predict what it will likely become. We are (or should be) prized for the ability to analyze a situation and select a course suited to the client's needs.

In most fields the competent strive to make what's difficult look effortless. Think of a gymnast doing a complicated routine. A dancer performing leaps and lifts. Your dentist installing a crown. They conceal the hours of training and practice needed to make what they do look easy. We should make the effort to write plain English so clearly and simply that the reader should think there's nothing to it. If clients believe they can do what we do, let them try. The best way to foster appreciation and understanding is by trying what looks easy and realizing that behind the apparent effortlessness is hard work, enormous skill, and mastery.

The best legal writing should be as good as the best journalism and literature. And it can be. Write plain English. Commit to clarity.

Then when someone says you "don't write like a lawyer," give me a call. I'll bring the champagne.

Exercises

Revise the following sentences so they're in the active voice. Then decide whether you think the revision is an improvement and, if so, why.

1. The Flag Protection Act of 1989 was passed by Congress in response to the decision of this Court in *Texas v. Johnson,* 1109 S.Ct. 2533 (1989).

2. During the period of employment, the employee shall be reimbursed by the employer for all reasonable and necessary out-of-pocket expenses incurred by the employee.

3. In early October 2003, plaintiffs were contacted by Entsol president Miller, who expressed interest in purchasing all rights to the invention.

4. Defendant was falsely incarcerated by the State of Maryland and held by directive of the State's Attorney General under a catch-all provision of the Patriot Act.

5. Until the decision of the Supreme Court in *Crawford,* the notion that the Sixth Amendment could be violated by hearsay was rejected by most of the circuit courts.

Revise the following sentences so they use concrete language, the active voice, and no superfluous words.

1. In the absence of a fully-executed writing, the common law provides that a deposit shall be returned in whole or in part where the agreement is timely canceled by the buyer; however, under the same or similar circumstances the seller shall be entitled to retain all or most of the security deposit where said seller fails to perform because of the buyer's breach.

2. The rationale for the aforesaid rule of the common law is based on the law's eagerness to encourage the parties to an agreement to formalize and memorialize their intentions and obligations in a fully executed writing, in the absence of which the common law will provide a remedy that may well prove unsatisfactory to all involved, and which would have been unnecessary but for the lack of a writing. Moreover, the common law will consider, as it must, whether there is a degree of fault on the breaching party to which the non-breaching party's failure to perform may be ascribed.

3. "There are many cases in which one party has assented to a definite bargain because of some antecedent error or computation that he has made."[31]

---

31. Arthur L. Corbin, *Corbin on Contracts* § 609 (one vol. ed., 1952).

4. "In any of its forms, the heart of cross-examination is the sequencing of short, clear, crafted statements that cannot plausibly be denied and which, in sequence, suggest an inference that supports, in one way or another, the cross-examiner's theory or theme of the case."[32]

5. "An[other] instance where conscious or calculating concern with deterrence will not motivate revenge is where the costs of taking revenge are less than the benefits in reducing the expected cost of future aggression."[33]

---

32. Robert P. Burns, *A Theory of the Trial* 59 (1999).
33. Richard A. Posner, *The Economics of Justice* 209 (1983).

Revise the following sentences to eliminate the adverbs while retaining or heightening the important information. Feel free to turn one sentence into two or more. Eliminate superfluous words and any passive constructions.

---

1. Incredibly, plaintiff — a highly experienced businessperson who has literally made millions of dollars from various ventures — disingenuously claims that she relied on defendant's merely oral representations that the non-assignability clause was unnecessary and should be removed.

2. Significantly, despite three formal requests, the government continues unfairly and unlawfully to withhold *Brady* material, which it utterly fails to deny it possesses, and which is materially necessary to the preparation of a fully adequate defense.

3. Clearly, Congress intended to create a substantially clearer and fairer method of fashioning sentences when it so carefully crafted the Guidelines so as to eliminate the need for judicial wisdom, prudence, clemency, experience, and discretion.

4. Astonishingly, at 4:00 a.m. police officers broke down the front door of the Conlons' apartment at 14 East 11th Street, forced the Conlons to lie on the floor, their hands cuffed behind their backs, and conducted a warrantless search that lasted over an hour and which yielded exactly nothing. Undoubtedly, the search would have continued, along with the startlingly horrid treatment of the Conlons, had one of the officers not been advised by a call from

the precinct that the anonymous tipster said the drugs and weapons were located at 14 East 12th Street, which means, incredibly, that the officers were warrantlessly searching the wrong apartment.

5. Astoundingly, the government intends to offer evidence of defendant McManus' 1986 assault conviction under Fred. R. Evid. 404(b), despite the fact that McManus and his co-defendants have been charged with insider trading. How the government intends to show that a conviction for assault, which is nearly two decades' old, tends to prove motive, intent, modus operandi, a common scheme, etc. in an insider trading case remains entirely mysterious — and completely impossible.

Place unnecessary words in the following passages in brackets. Re-read the passages to find out whether the meaning is clearer without the bracketed material. Re-read the material again, looking for additional words that may be placed in brackets. Then, if you like, rewrite the passages without the bracketed material and compare the revised versions to the originals.

1. The Act represents "an avowed departure from the rules of the common law." Recognizing the special need to protect railroaders from the inherently dangerous nature of their work, Congress enacted the Act to shift part of the "human overhead" of doing business from the employees to their employers. The Act strips employers of their common law defenses of assumption of the risk and contributory negligence as a bar to recovery and abandons general concepts of proximate cause.

2. "The work of deciding cases goes on every day in hundreds of courts throughout the land. Any judge, one might suppose, would find it easy to describe the process which he had followed a thousand times and more. Nothing could be farther from the truth. Let some intelligent layman ask him to explain: he will not go very far before taking refuge in the excuse that the language of the craftsman is unintelligible to those untutored in the craft. Such an excuse may cover with a semblance of respectability an ignominious retreat. It will hardly serve to still the pricks of curiosity and conscience."[34]

---

34. Benjamin N. Cardozo, *The Nature of the Judicial Process* 9 (1949).

3. "In this case [a libel suit] there must be a new trial. We shall state the grounds on which we come to this conclusion, and shall discuss such of the rulings as dealt with questions which are likely to come up again. Some matters not likely to recur we shall pass over. The first question which we shall consider is raised by the presiding judge's refusal to rule that the articles were privileged. The requests referred to each article as a whole. Each article contained direct and indirect allegations of fact touching the plaintiff, and highly detrimental to him, charging him with being a party to alleged frauds in the New York customs-house. Some or all of these allegations we must take to be false. Therefore, the ruling asked was properly refused."[35]

4. "The original Fair Labor Standards Act passed in 1938 specifically excluded the States and their political subdivisions from its coverage. In 1974, however, Congress enacted the most recent of a series of broadening amendments to the Act. By these amendments Congress has extended the minimum wage and maximum hour provisions to almost all public employees employed by the States and by their various subdivisions. Appellants in these cases include individual cities and States, the National League of Cities, and the National Governors' Conference; they brought an action in the District Court for the District of Columbia which challenged the validity of the 1974 amendments. They asserted in effect that when Congress sought to apply the Fair Labor Standards Act provisions virtually across the board to employees of state and municipal governments it 'infringed a constitutional prohibition' running in favor of the States As States. The gist of their complaint was not that the conditions of employment of such public

---

35. *Burt v. Advertiser Newspaper Co.*, 154 Mass. 238, 28 N.E. 1 (1891) (Holmes, J.).

employees were beyond the scope of the commerce power had those employees been employed in the private sector but that the established constitutional doctrine of intergovernmental immunity consistently recognized in a long series of our cases affirmatively prevented the exercise of this authority in the manner which Congress chose in the 1974 amendments."[36]

5. "The District Court granted respondent's motion for summary judgment. The court stated that scientific evidence is admissible only if the principle upon which it is based is 'sufficiently established to have general acceptance in the field to which it belongs' ... The court concluded that petitioners' evidence did not meet this standard. Given the vast body of epidemiological data concerning Bendectin, the court held, expert opinion which is not based on epidemiological evidence is not admissible to establish causation. Thus, the animal-cell studies, live-animal studies, and chemical-structure analyses on which petitioners had relied could not raise by themselves a reasonably disputable jury regarding causation ... Petitioners' epidemiological analyses, based as they were on recalculations of data in previously published studies that had found no causal link between the drug and birth defects, were ruled to be inadmissible because they had not been published or subjected to peer review."[37]

---

36. *Nat'l League of Cities v. Usery*, 96 S.Ct. 2465, 2467 (1976) (footnotes omittted), overruled by *Garcia v. San Antonio Metro. Trans. Auth.*, 469 U.S. 528 (1985).
37. *Daubert v. Merrell Dow Parms., Inc.*, 113 S.Ct. 2786, 2794 (1993) (citations omitted).

Revise the following sentences to eliminate double- and single-negatives.

1. Expert opinion which is not based on epidemiological evidence is not admissible to establish causation.

2. The complaint is not a model of clarity.

3. Defendant's testimony, though not unpersuasive, was apparently not credible to the jurors, as they did not find defendant not guilty.

4. Failure to deliver the goods seasonably shall not constitute a breach of this contract where said failure is not caused by Solvex's negligence or willfulness.

5. Decedent did not disinherit her issue; she simply did not leave them any portion of her estate, the whole of which she left to her gecko, Marlon.

Notes

Appendix

Mock-Article in Laurence Sterne's *Tristram Shandy*
(*see* Chapter 5)

From Laurence Sterne, *The Life and Opinions of Tristram Shandy* 82–89
(vol. 1, 1st ed. 1760 [1759]).

And this Indenture further witnesseth. That the
said *Walter Shandy,* merchant, in consideration of
the said intended marriage to be had, and, by God's
blessing, to be well and truly solemnized and con-
summated between the said *Walter Shandy* and
Elizabeth Mollineux aforesaid, and divers other
good and valuable causes and considerations him
thereunto specially moving,—doth grant, covenant,
condescend, consent, conclude, bargain, and fully
agree to and with *John Dixon* and *James Turner,*
Esqrs. the above-named trustees, &c. &c.—to
wit,—That in case it should hereafter so fall out,
chance, happen, or otherwise come to pass,—That
the said *Walter Shandy,* merchant, shall have left off
business before the time or times, that the said

Elizabeth Mollineux shall, according to the course wise, have left off bearing and bring forth children;—and that, in consequence of the said *Walter Shandy* having so left off business, shall, in despight, and against the free will, consent, and good-liking of the said *Elizabeth Mollineux,*—make a departure from the city of London, in order to retire to, and dwell upon, his estate at Shandy-Hall, in the country of——, or at any other country seat, castle, hall, mansion-house, messuage, or grainge-house, now purchased, or hereafter to be purchased, or upon any part of parcel thereof:—That then, and as often as the said *Elizabeth Mollineux* shall happen to be enceint with child or children severally and lawfully begot, or to be begotten, upon the body of the said *Elizabeth Mollineux* during her said coverture,——he the said *Walter Shandy* shall, at his own proper cost and charges, and out of his own proper monies, upon good and reasonable notice, which is hereby agreed to be within six weeks of her the said *Elizabeth Mollineux*'s full reckoning, or time of supposed and computed delivery,—pay, or cause to be paid, the sum of one hundred and twenty pounds of good and lawful money, to *John Dixon* and *James Turner,* Esqrs. or assigns,—upon TRUST and confidence, and for and unto the use and uses, intent, end, and purpose following:—𝔗𝔥𝔞𝔱 𝔦𝔰 𝔱𝔬 𝔰𝔞𝔶.—That the said sum of one hundred and twenty pounds shall be paid into the hands of the said *Elizabeth Mollineux,* or to be otherwise applied by them the said trustees, for the well and truly hiring of one coach, with able and sufficient horses, to carry and convey the body of the said *Elizabeth Mollineux* and the child or children which she shall be then and there enceint and pregnant with,—unto the city of *London;* and for the further paying and defraying of all other incidental costs, charges, and expences whatsoever,—in and about, and for, and relating to her said intended delivery and lying-in, in the said city or suburbs thereof. And that the said *Elizabeth Mollineux* shall and may, from time to time, and at all such time and times as are here covenanted and agreed upon,—peaceably and quietly hire the said coach and horses, and have free ingress, egress, and regress throughout her journey, in and from the said coach, according to the tenor, true intent, and meaning of these presents, without any let, suit, trouble, disturbance, molestation, discharge, hin-derance, forfeiture, eviction, vexation, interrup-tion, or incumberance whatsoever.—And that it shall moreover be lawful to and for the said *Eliza-beth Mollineux,* from time to time, and as oft or often as she shall well and truly be advanced in her said pregnancy, to the time heretofore stipulated and agreed upon,—to live and reside in such place or places, and in such family or families, and with such relations, friends, and other persons within the said city of *London,* as she, at her own will and pleasure, notwithstanding her present coverture, and as if she was a *femme sole* and unmarried,— shall think fit.—𝕬𝕟𝖉 𝖙𝖍𝖎𝖘 𝕴𝖓𝖉𝖊𝖓𝖙𝖚𝖗𝖊 𝖋𝖚𝖗𝖙𝖍𝖊𝖗 𝖜𝖎𝖙𝖓𝖊𝖘𝖘𝖊𝖙𝖍. That for the more effectually carrying of the said covenant into execution, the said *Walter Shandy,* merchant, doth hereby grant, bargain, sell, release, and confirm unto the said *John Dixon* and *James Turner,* Esqrs. their heirs, executors, and assigns, in their actual possession, now being by virtue of an indenture of bargain and sale for a year to them the said *John Dixon* and *James Turner,* Esqrs. by him the said *Walter Shandy,* merchant, thereof made; which said bargain and sale for a year, bears date the day next before the date of these presents, and by force and virtue of the statute for transferring of uses into possession, ——𝕬𝖑𝖑 that the manor and lordship of *Shandy* in the country of——, with all the rights, members, and appurtenances thereof; and all and every the messuages, houses, buildings, barns, stables, orchards, gardens, backsides, tofts, crofts, garths, cottages, lands, meadows, feedings, pastures, marshes, commons, woods, underwoods, drains, fisheries, waters, and water-courses;—together with all rents, reversions, services, annuities, fee-farms, knights fees, views of frank-pledge, escheats, reliefs, mines, quarries, goods and chattels of felons and fugitives, felons of themselves, and put in exigent, deodands, free warrens, and all other royalties and seignories, rights and jurisdictions, privileges and hereditaments whatsoever. ———And also the advowson, donation, presentation and free disposition of the rectory or parsonage of *Shandy* aforesaid, and all and every the tenths, tythes, glebe-lands———In three words, ———"My mother was to lay in, (if she chose it) in *London*."

Suggested Reading

Barzun, Jacques. *Simple & Direct.* 1985

Bernstein, Theodore M. *The Careful Writer.* 1965.

Flesch, Rudolf. *How to Write, Speak, and Think More Effectively.* 1960.

----------. *The Art of Readable Writing.* 1967.

Garner, Bryan A. *The Elements of Legal Style.* 1991.

----------. *A Dictionary of Modern Legal Usage.* 1995.

----------. *The Winning Brief.* 1999.

----------. *The Oxford Dictionary of American Usage and Style.* 2000.

----------. *Legal Writing in Plain English.* 2001.

----------. *The Redbook: A Manual of Legal Style.* 2002.

Orwell, George. *A Collection of Essays.* 1981.

Strunk, William, Jr. & E.B. White. *The Elements of Style.* 3rd ed. 1979.

Wydick, Richard C. *Plain English for Lawyers.* 4th ed. 1998.

Zinsser, William. *On Writing Well.* 6th ed. 1998.

Index